Cheat Codes
to High School

Written by a Student

Preston Pierott

Acknowledgments

A special thank you to my editors who generously sacrificed their time to help me: Deidra Perry, Anthony Wilson, and Zack O'Neil. To my family whose love and support continues to strengthen and encourage me; especially my parents whose love, discipline, guidance, and wisdom has shaped me into the man I am today. Thanks most of all to God who has blessed me greatly; without whom I would accomplish nothing.

ISBN-13: 978-0-692-51858-8

To my brother, the valedictorian before me, whose example inspired me to work my hardest for a sheet of paper. Well to be fair it's a nice sheet of paper.

Table of Contents

Part 1: Introduction

CHAPTER 1

POPULAR MISCONCEPTION

Valedictorian and salutatorian are the two students who graduate with the highest scores -I had the highest. Many people assume that becoming valedictorian meant I was the smartest student in the school, when the truth is I was not. There were many other students who had the potential of becoming valedictorian. Many students had much higher SAT scores than I. Then how did I manage to become so successful? Well, there are many factors to that; however, in short, I made up my mind of what I was going to do from the beginning, I worked hard, I listened, and I played smart. In order to be successful in anything you have to be hardworking and disciplined; you cannot be one or the other. In this book, I will guide you on your road through high school. If you listen to my instructions, though it may not be guaranteed that you will achieve everything that I have, there is no reason why you should not graduate as a successful student.

Some have the misconception that having a high intelligence is the only key to success. This is not true. Success comes through hard work, perseverance, and more importantly the willingness to listen and learn quickly. Do not get me wrong: having a high intelligence can be a great help, but it does not guarantee success. One individual student in my class was brilliant. He almost scored perfectly on his SAT on his first attempt. However, he was so lazy he barely made it into the top 10% of the class. He had every potential of becoming a competitor for valedictorian.

Laziness can fall upon anyone however. Throughout my years in high school I found that one of the reasons many students were not ranked higher was not because they had a low intelligence, it was the fact that many students did not have the will to work as hard as they could have. In my experience I have noticed that one of the main reasons behind this was due to the fact that many of them did not take high school seriously enough early on. Of course, I still had competition from those that worked just as hard as I did, however, there could have been plenty more.

You have to ask yourself, "Do I want to work hard? Do I really want to do what it takes to be successful? Am I willing to sacrifice my free time to make it to the top?" To be successful, you will have to give up more of your free time to studying, and you will have many sleepless nights. That does not mean you will no longer be able to have any fun (you would go crazy otherwise), it only means that you will not have as much. If you are serious enough to commit, the results will be worth it! Whether you are an average mind or a brilliant mind, if you listen to my instructions, and be consistent, not only will you become successful

overall, but you will be on track to reaching your

full potential.

PART 2:
PREPARING FOR
HIGH SCHOOL

Chapter 2

New Beginnings

Ideally, it is best that you begin reading this book at the beginning of your eighth grade year. One reason is because you are offered high school credit classes during this time; how well you do in those classes will affect your high school success. The other reason is because you are getting ready to enter a whole new world: high school. You may have to throw out any negative behaviors and ideas that you once had; this is not something you can just change in one day. It requires focus, preparation, and dedication. You will have to be prepared before you start your first day of school.

Freshman year is arguably the most important year of your high school years. You are building a foundation for your GPA (grade point average). If you are not serious, and perform poorly you could permanently damage your GPA. Yes, high school is a fun and an exciting experience; however, many freshmen do not get past that part. Sadly, some focus on having fun rather than putting in enough work and effort as they should. Do you know what happens after that? It will not be until their junior or senior year that they start to wish they had worked harder when they first started. Every year juniors and seniors say this because they make the same mistake of blowing off their freshman year. Your junior and senior years are where both your class ranking and GPA start to become etched in stone. By then, it is almost impossible to dramatically increase your GPA. This information will more than likely be given to you by multiple sources. Teachers, administrator, and even upperclassmen have or will warn you of slacking off your first year. There will still be those who choose not to listen, and they will warn the new students not to make the same mistake; yet the cycle will continue. In your first year, you will either start off digging yourself into a hole or you will build a strong foundation for a successful high school experience.

CHAPTER 3
SUMMER
ASSIGNMENTS

As you are preparing to enjoy your summer you have more than likely received or will receive a summer assignment from your English teachers (or possibly from other classes). DO NOT put it off until the end of the summer. I know what you are thinking, "Who gives homework over the summer?!" Personally I agree with you one-hundred percent. It is a total buzzkill; however, your teachers are not doing it to be evil per se. They are not doing it because they love to see their student's miserable (though some might), they are actually trying to prepare you for the work you will be doing when school starts. The assignment has more value than a simple grade. In my experience I have found that teachers are also trying to figure out what kind of student you are. They are looking to see if you actually read all material that was assigned, whether or not you followed all directions, how much effort and thought you put into your work, and whether or not you went the extra mile to complete the extra credit (if they offered it). All of these aspects can factor into a teachers mind. Once your teacher hands back your assignments graded, that teacher may have already begun deciding in their minds what kind of student you are.

You might be wondering, "Why should I put that much effort into one assignment? After all it is only one teacher anyway." First impressions are extremely important. They can be long lasting and sometimes permanent. You want to put your best foot forward. There is something else you need to learn: one class can be the deciding factor on what your GPA and overall ranking will be. So no matter what class you are taking, who the teacher might be, you always want to do your very best.

How do you plan to complete the assignment?

Because I am a student that loves summer just as much as you, I recommend enjoying your first few weeks of summer vacation. Hang out with your friends, play video games, do whatever you do to enjoy your summer. That is something some adults might not advise you to do, but it is perfectly fine. Some teachers and other adults will tell you finish your work first and then enjoy your summer. Let's be realistic, if you are like me, the last thing you want to do right after finishing school is more work! This is the reason I recommend you relax and enjoy yourself for the first few weeks of summer before you do anything.

After that, towards the middle of summer, you need to begin working on your summer assignment(s). Now you have two options (1) finish your entire assignments(s) in a week or two. This is for those students, like me, who do their best work when they start and do not stop until completion. It is like eating your vegetables first so that you can enjoy your favorite part of the meal last. This means that you will only spend a small part of your summer doing work and you have the rest of the summer to relax. (2) Do just a little of the assignment each week until the end of summer. Now this takes both good planning and dedication. You cannot slack off once. If you do, chances are you will do it again and then again. Before you know, it will be the end of summer and you only have half the assignment completed. If that is the case, you will more than likely slop the rest of the assignment together to complete it; however, sloppy work will not look good to your teacher. If you choose to go this route plan well and stick to that plan.

Hopefully by the end of summer you would have completed your assignment(s), followed every direction, put a lot of thought into it, and even completed the extra credit. As you continue reading, you will learn that while doing your best in class academically is important, there are other factors that are just as important.

CHAPTER 4

THE PURPOSE OF HIGH SCHOOL

Now that you are in high school, there are several things that you need to know. You may think that high school is about starting over, being the best person you can be, and making new friends. While that is all a part of the high school experience it is not the purpose of high school. Many students do not fully understand the purpose of high school until their junior year; sadly some do not figure it out until their senior year. In either case this may be too late. Fortunately for you I am going to shed light on things that can benefit you even before you start high school. The purpose of high school is to develop a good reputation as a student so that colleges will accept you. The purpose of high school is to get into college. I will take it a step further and say that the purpose of high school is to get into college while paying the least amount of money out of your family's or your own pocket. Almost everything you do in high school will have an effect on your reputation as a student whether you realize it or not. By the end of your four years of high school, colleges will look at what you have accomplished. So what are the main factors that affect your "reputation"? I will explain them in this section.

Chapter 5

GPA

What is a GPA?

GPA stands for "grade point average". In short, it is the average of all your grades in high school. Every year your GPA will change depending on how well your scores are each year. When you make good grades your GPA increases, and if you make poor grades your GPA decreases. In some cases, your final GPA will be given to you at the end of the first semester of your senior year.

Your final GPA is one of the most important aspects of your high school career that colleges look at. Your personal goal should be to get the highest GPA possible by the end of your senior year.

Many colleges have required GPA's students must have in order to be eligible for acceptance. Check the requirements of the colleges you want to attend. I suggest looking up at least four different colleges; you can never be sure who will accept you. Check the requirements yearly because they are subject to change.

How do GPA's work?

Well now that you have a general idea of what a GPA is, let me explain how it works. As I mentioned previously, your GPA is based upon how high or how low your grades are. Each grade you receive in a class grants a number of points.

Depending on whether you take a regular or advanced class, that class will be graded on either a 4.0 or 5.0 scale. Each scale represents the highest number of points you can potentially receive in a class. In many cases the 4.0 scale is associated with "regular" classes and the 5.0 scale is associated with "advanced" (honors) classes.

If you are taking a regular class and earn an A, you will receive 4 points for that class. The number of points cycles down with each letter grade. So if you earn a B in one class then you will receive 3 points for that class. If you earn a C you receive 2 points. If you earn a D you receive 1 point. If you receive an 'F' you will not get any points at all; you do not receive points for failing.

You may or may not know this yet but there are "advanced" (honors) classes. These are classes that have "AP" or "Pre-AP" in front of the subject that you may be taking. For example, on your schedule it may read something like, "Pre-AP Algebra" or "AP US History". "AP" stands for "Advanced Placement". These classes are more difficult than regular classes. They require a lot more work and effort. However, these are the classes that can help boost your GPA as high as possible. If you receive an A in an advanced class you receive 5 points instead of 4. You may not think that is much of a difference, but it can weigh heavily on your GPA. The more advanced classes you take, the higher your GPA can be. For example, if you were to earn a B in an advanced class you would receive 4 points; that is exactly like getting an A in a regular class. It is the same if you were to earn a C in an advanced class; you would receive 3 points (equivalent to a B in a regular class). If you were to earn a D in an advanced class then you would receive 2 points (equivalent to a C in a regular class). If you are thinking that if you earn an 'F' in an advanced class you can still get 1 point you do not; you do not receive any points for failing a class in either case. Taking advanced courses increase the chances of maximizing your GPA. In order to get a perfect 4.0 average by taking all regular classes you would have to get straight A's in all your classes. If you were to take advanced classes you could still earn a 4.0 or even higher without straight A's every year.

Depending on your high school, the point system may vary slightly. Perhaps your school utilizes the "plus and minus" system (A+, A-, and B+, etc.). It is possible that your school has a separate point system between honors and AP classes. In any case, the main idea remains the same: the higher your grades are in the most advanced classes, the higher your GPA will be. Double check your schools point system so that you will be able to personally calculate your GPA accurately.

AP Exams

There is a slight down side to taking AP classes. Even though pre-AP and AP classes may have the same point value, if you have an AP class you have to take what is called an AP exam at the end of the year. It is a timed exam that tests your overall knowledge of a particular class. I said it was a "slight" down side because it is an extra exam you have to take; in actuality it is a great benefit for you in the future. The good news is that if you pass the AP exam, depending on the college you select, you could actually receive college credit for that class. For example, if you were to pass the AP World History exam you would not have to take that in college; this can save you hundreds of dollars. If you pass multiple AP exams you could be saving yourself thousands of dollars. Keep in mind that some colleges may require you to score higher than the bare minimum passing score in order to receive college credit.

I recommend taking these tests seriously because it provides an excellent opportunity. Despite their importance, AP exams have ZERO effect on your GPA. It will not even negatively affect your college application if you were to fail any of your AP exams; so do not stress yourself out if you fail any of them. If you are still worried let me help you out. In all four years of high school, I did not pass a single AP exam. Most of my fellow AP classmates passed at least one exam. Like I explained before, I was not the smartest student in my school. I never did as well with timed tests. Despite that, I still became valedictorian. Do not allow that to be an excuse not to do your best; it is a rare opportunity that you should take full advantage of.

Unweighted vs Weighted GPA

In order to receive your GPA (generally that can be done at your registrar's office) you will need to request what is called a transcript. Your transcript is similar to a receipt that lists all your classes and the grades you received for each one of them. At the bottom of your transcript you may find that there is a "weighted" and an "unweighted" score. Your unweighted score treats all your classes (including advanced) as regular classes; this score is not as significant and should not distract you. Your weighted score averages all your scores as they should by distinguishing advanced from regular; this is the score that matters to colleges. Later in this book I will explain how to create your schedule between regular and advanced classes so that you can boost your GPA much higher than everyone else's.

CHAPTER 6

CLASS RANKING

What is Class Ranking?

Your GPA and class ranking are closely

related. If you have ever played online games, you

have the ability to see where you are ranked in

comparison with the rest of the world based on

certain skills. Your class ranking is essentially the

same thing except you are ranked with your entire

class based upon your GPA. The higher your GPA,

the higher your ranking, and the lower your GPA,

the lower your ranking. Ranking is not as important to colleges as your GPA. There are not many benefits to ranking unless your ranking is relatively high. Students often have more opportunities if they rank high and have a high GPA (this includes scholarship opportunities).

Valedictorian and salutatorian are not the only high ranking positions. Every class is ranked among percentages (e.g. top 10%, top 15% etc.) that depend on the number of students and your GPA in comparison to the rest of your class. In Texas, for example, if your class ranking is within the top 10% of your class, you will automatically be accepted into any public college in the state of Texas (as of 2016). If you do not attend a high school in Texas, more than likely this policy will not apply to you;

however, being in the top range of your class can still lead to other opportunities while being an asset on your college application.

CHAPTER 7

SAT AND ACT

What is the SAT?

The SAT is a difficult timed test that tests your overall knowledge in reading, writing, and math. It is basically like the standardized test taken at the end of every year except it is more difficult. The test itself is not free. Although there is no pass or fail score, you must receive the required score issued by the college you wish to attend in order to be considered for acceptance. The highest number of points you can receive is 1600 (as of 2016). If you managed to receive a perfect score on your SAT and your GPA is decent, you can almost literally get into any college you want; this includes Ivy League colleges like Harvard and Yale. That does not mean you have to get a perfect score to get into the college of your dreams however. It is extremely rare for students to receive perfect scores. This test exists because it is difficult to identify exemplary students by using GPA and ranking from hundreds of different schools. The SAT is designed to distinguish exemplary students. Doing extremely well on the SAT opens up more scholarship opportunities and access to more colleges.

Some argue that you cannot really study for this test. I completely disagree. People that say this and or agree with this, like I did, often are those who look for an excuse not to try to prepare for the test. If there is a test for something you can prepare for it. I, unfortunately, learned this too late. I did not do as well and in the process I missed out on some incredible scholarship opportunities. If you plan well, you can avoid making this mistake and be far more successful than I was. For more information on the SAT see either your counselor and or go online to *SAT.collegeboard.com.*

What is the ACT?

ACT stands for "American College Test". The ACT is similar to the SAT, but not as popular. Unlike the SAT, however, the highest number of points you can receive is a 36 (as of 2016). The test is a slightly different format, but has the same concept. Some claim that the ACT is easier than the SAT. I recommend taking both to see which one you fare better in.

Like the SAT, the ACT can be just as necessary to get into college. Colleges will accept either SAT or ACT scores. Whichever tests you decide to take colleges have requirement scores for both. In order to be considered in the acceptance process, you must satisfy those requirements. Again, check the requirements of the colleges you wish to attend. For more information on the ACT speak with your counselor and or go online to *actstudent.org.*

How to Prepare for SAT and ACT

More than likely you have heard the popular phrase when referring to the SAT, "You either know it or you don't." You can practically apply that to any test during test time. When you start a test you either know the information by then or you do not. The phrase should not to be used as an excuse not to spend time studying and preparing for it. As I previously stated, if there is a test for something then you can prepare for it. Preparing for the SAT and ACT is extra work; however, it is well worth it. There are individuals who are naturally good at test taking; nevertheless, you can still benefit more by preparing for it.

There are actually classes, outside of school, that you can take to prepare for the test; you will have to pay for these classes. I wish I was aware of this beforehand and had taken advantage of it. There are also SAT/ACT prep books available for purchase which are full of tips and sample problems to practice with. Make sure you purchase the most updated version.

I recommend you begin searching for classes and purchasing your book the second semester of your sophomore year. Beginning around this time helps you to build up to taking the pre-SAT and or pre-ACT by the end of your junior year. The pre-SAT and the pre-ACT are simply the test you take to predict how well you would do on the real test. It is not mandatory to take, but it is a great way to learn where you stand without having to pay extra for the actual test. Having taken the pre-test your junior year you will know what you need to focus on and prepare for the actual test(s) your senior year. During the first semester of your senior year take the SAT and ACT as many times as you can afford to, or at least enough to meet the required score for the colleges you wish to attend. Check the available times in which you can sign up for the exam. The goal is to receive the highest score possible by the end of December so you can prepare to send off your college applications.

This is not the only time table you have to prepare for your test. If you want to have your desired score sooner so that you can send off your early college applications by the deadline, then you can skip the pre-tests and instead take the actual test(s) your junior year. Gauge it how you want to. If you are still unclear of what is best for you, see your counselor for further advice. As for any test, make sure you get enough rest, do not cram the night before, and eat a healthy but light breakfast the morning of.

CHAPTER 8

WHY IS YOUR GPA, RANKING, SAT AND ACT SUCH A BIG DEAL?

Colleges are primarily concerned with GPA (which is combined with ranking) and SAT/ACT scores. Colleges are competitive! This is especially true if your goal is to be accepted into high ranking (Ivy League) colleges such as Harvard, Princeton, or Columbia University. You cannot have sloppy scores. Even if you are the best athlete in the country, if your grades are not good enough you still will not get into a college that requires much higher scores than what you have; this means that if your scores are too low you run the risk of not receiving any athletic scholarship. Given that, make these four important years of your life count!

Another reason these are important is that it factors in to what scholarships you will receive. The higher your scores, the more scholarships you will be applicable for. The more scholarships you get the less you or your parents have to pay for your college education. That means, unlike many college students, you could potentially graduate with zero debt (as I did). You will really appreciate that when you are older and trying to buy a new car and or home. There are too many students who are drowned in debt from college loans when they graduate. For some, it takes many years until they are able to pay them off. You want to acquire as many scholarships as you can.

Chapter 9

How to Boost Your GPA

Now that you have an idea of what colleges look for, you will need to know how to set everything in motion. Though working hard was a huge part of my success, if I had not scheduled my classes correctly I would not have become valedictorian. I owe that all to my older brother who provided me with the information on how to do so.

He was valedictorian before me, and he figured out how to arrange his schedule to help give him an edge. Scheduling your classes correctly will be the single-most important attribute to your academic success for the next four years.

If you are starting eighth grade, you may be offered high school credit classes (such as Algebra 1). I recommend not taking those classes for two reasons: (1) Students tend not do as well as they need to and or the class itself can hinder their high school success (2) you want to reserve as many classes for high school to fill up your schedule. Even if you were to make an A in those classes, (if you are trying to compete for the highest position and it counts as a regular class in high school) it could set you back. Taking high school classes early will not benefit you as much. Given this information, it may benefit you to avoid such classes before high school.

Depending on how enrollment works, your parents may have already received a schedule request form before you graduate from middle school. More than likely they are not going to know what you will need, and as a result, you will be given a standard schedule. Perhaps your parents chose some of the right classes but it still may not be correct. If this does occur, be sure to have it fixed the summer before you start school.

Why is it imperative that your schedule is correct the summer before school starts? Having an incorrect schedule can potentially become a problem at the beginning of the year. Depending on how large and organized your school is, there could be several students with schedules that they do not want or need; it could possibly take weeks to fix them all. This will lead to unnecessary time spent in classes you do not need, which causes you to fall behind in classes you actually need. You do not want to wait until then because it is still not guaranteed that it will be fixed the first time. It also does not guarantee that there will be enough space for you in the classes you need. Even in the future, when you have already completed your schedule request form, you will still need to visit your school and make sure that it is correct.

To complete your schedule quickly, correctly, and with the least amount of stress, you are going to need your parent or guardian. Let me tell you a secret that many schools will be upset at me for saying: schools are more likely to move a lot faster when your parents are present. You will need them throughout your four years to make sure your schedule is always in order. About 3 weeks before school starts take your parent/guardian with you to school, find out who does your schedule, and visit that administrator personally. You will want to see them directly because they are the ones who will have to change your schedule and you want to develop a good relationship early on. Depending on how large your school is, it is easy for those in authority to not know you (after all they may see hundreds of kids every day). Getting to know your counselor (or whoever the administrator is who is assigned to you) and them getting to know you makes any future meetings run smoother.

What classes to Choose

Well you are now sitting with your administrator/counselor to make sure you are signed up for the right classes. Now what? Well that all depends on you. You will need to define your academic goals to determine how far you want to go. Are you motivated enough to work as hard as you can? If you are not motivated enough to maintain focus you can sign up for the right classes, but still perform poorly.

If you are motivated and driven to do your best, here is what you need to do. As I mentioned above, Pre-AP and AP classes count more than regular classes. In short, you want to fill your schedule up with only advanced classes. When you are trying to maximize your GPA, even if you were to get an A in a regular class it will still lower your GPA. If you are having problems understanding this here is an example: if you were to average two 100's and one 90 together, though that 90 is a good grade, because it is lower than those other 100's it drops your average. If you are trying to get the highest GPA that you possibly can so that you can rank high, then it is imperative that you avoid regular classes as much as possible. There are some instances where you will have no choice but to take a regular class in order to graduate (like gym and health classes). However, some schools will offer Pre-AP/AP versions of those mandatory classes. Ask your counselor if your school provides them. If not, do not worry about it; you are not at any disadvantage if the rest of your classmates have to do the same, however, try to reserve those classes for the last semester of your senior year if you can.

Your GPA is only affected by the first three and a half years of high school (the last semester of your senior year will not count against your GPA); of course you must still pass those classes to graduate. A great way to help you do this is by asking for a listing of all the classes you need to take in order to graduate; by doing so allows you to plan which classes you can reserve for the second semester of your senior year. Sometimes you may not have any other options but to take some before your senior year. I had to take two semesters of P.E so I took one semester early on and saved the other semester for the second semester of my senior year.

If you do decide to take all Pre-AP/AP classes, keep in mind that these are very difficult, or rather, more difficult than regular classes. Your goal is not to do "ok" in these classes. Your goal is to get an A to maximize your GPA. This may require you to stay up late many nights to study, complete assignments, and attend tutorial sessions to help you grasp the material faster. You will not have as much time to play around like the rest of your friends. I know this seems dull, but the results will be worth it. Trust me, your peers, towards graduation, are going to tell you that they wished they had done what you did.

Taking all pre-AP and AP courses can exhaust you. To help alleviate your work load, I recommend that you take one non-credit course. For me, I was either an office worker or a library assistant every year. This allowed me both extra study time as well as an opportunity to make connections with other administrators and teachers. Though you do not get any credit for such a course, having it may benefit you more than taking another class. Taking another class may take too much of your time resulting in lower scores for all your classes. This way, you have more time to focus on building up your grades for the rest of your courses. To have the opportunity to take such a course is another reason why you want to meet with your administrator personally in the summer to adjust your schedule. Simply ask them if there is a non-credit course you can take; you may not receive a more direct and reliable answer from anyone else.

If you do not have the mind set to do well then you definitely will not. Now at times, you might fall short of your goal of getting an A (sometimes even a B), however, as long as you know you put one-hundred percent into your work, not having any regrets that you stayed up watching a show or playing a game when you should have been studying, you have nothing to feel bad about; you did your best! Your main focus is on your semester average grade anyway. Even if on one report card you get lower than you want, you still have the remainder of the semester to build up your grade. If you realize that you could use a few points to help boost your grade do not be afraid to ask for extra credit from your teachers.

If you are still worried about whether or not you can handle AP courses let me say this: unless you have a medical condition that prevents your learning process (I am NOT talking about "ADHD".

Both the salutatorian of our class and I had ADHD),

I believe there is no reason you cannot survive those

classes with at least a B. You are much smarter than

you think. My parents did not believe I could handle

it initially, but I made up my mind to be successful

and I surprised both them and even myself.

Filling up your schedule with all pre-AP and

AP classes is not the only way to go. I did that in

order to become valedictorian. If you have no

interest in ranking that high then you can choose to

mix in regular classes with advanced classes. As I

mentioned in the beginning, the purpose of high

school is to get into college; having all advanced

courses is not necessary to do that. In this instance

your objective should be to try and get a 4.0 GPA

by the end of your senior year. A 4.0 is still very

impressive to colleges. A 4.0 is like having an A overall. You could get a 4.0 by getting all A's in all your classes (if you were to take all regular). Though you can do it, it can be hard still to maintain straight A's all around. Try to combine your schedule with half regular and the other advanced. You will still want to make A's in your regular classes. Because advanced classes count as more, you could still get a 4.0 without having to get an A in all of your classes. Even if you were to get a B in a regular class, your advanced class, if you do well enough, could recover you.

I personally believe you can take all advanced courses and do well, but do what you feel is more comfortable. It all depends on how far you want to go and how much work you want to put in.

Keep in mind, the more you challenge yourself and the more that you meet those challenges, the better the reward. Though you do not have to load your schedule up with difficult classes, by doing well in them, more opportunities will open up for you. Do not be afraid to challenge yourself, the results may surpass your expectations as well as those around you.

Dual Credit Classes

Dual credit classes live up to its name. By taking a dual credit class, you receive the credit for both high school and a credit for college! Depending on how many of these classes you take, you could start college and be a year ahead. If you were to combine both dual credit classes with passing your AP exams you could advance further ahead in college, saving yourself thousands of dollars in the process.

As with many great things, there is a draw back. In some cases a dual credit class counts as a regular class. If you are trying to become valedictorian, salutatorian, or even top 10, taking these classes will kill your GPA. Of course your GPA will still look good, but when you are competing for top positions, these classes could still set you behind significantly. Though I wanted to take these classes, I steered clear from them because of this. If you do not mind this draw back, then I recommend taking as many of these courses as you can. Speak to your counselor for further details.

Chapter 10

How to Study

This is a topic which can vary from student to student. While in high school you are going to have to determine what studying methods are going to work for you. The most important factor that helped me to study and do as well as I did was not having TV. We all know that spell TV can cast on you; once you start watching one show you want to see what is next. My parents did not want that distraction for my brother and I so they made sure that it was not a part of our lives at an early age. They did still provide us with VHS movies, DVD's, and video games.

Even then my parents had a rule that we could not play games or watch movies during the school week. On Friday's, when we got home, we could relax. On Saturdays we had to finish our homework first before we could relax and have fun. This may seem extreme to you now, but since this was how everything worked from the beginning it was normal for us. With my parents producing two valedictorians you cannot argue with the results.

I am not telling you to throw out your TV. What I do want you to take from this is how to have discipline. Cut out from watching TV and playing games during the week, and dedicate your week to studying. I guarantee you that your grades will be significantly higher this way.

I understand that being this disciplined is very difficult for those who were not brought up this way. Understanding this, I will make one slight modification. Do not play video games at all during the week (it is too easy to lose track of time). If you are not in athletics or any other extracurricular activities after school then watch only two episodes of whatever you want to watch. If you are in athletics or any other extracurricular activity (including any religious activities) after school, watch only one episode a day. Try alternating studying and watching your episodes; it will help you to study first and then give yourself a break.

If you really want to do your best, I would suggest you go with my first recommendation. It is just too tempting to watch another show right afterward (especially when you do not feel like doing work). Whether you choose my original or modified recommendation, Fridays, when you get home, you can relax and watch/play whatever you want. Saturdays, however, you must complete all assignments before you relax. We had to do this because we had church on Sunday. If you do not have religious events during the weekend, on Saturdays you can begin studying and then take short breaks every couple hours of studying. If you manage to get all your work completed by Saturday, you will have the entire Sunday to yourself. Again, you are going to have to figure out what works best for you.

Studying while having a Job

What does having a job have to do with studying? Everything! It can negatively impact your studying ability. If at all possible, avoid getting a job. I know some of you may have family circumstances that my require you to, that is fine; it may be extremely hard to do your best. In this instance, you cannot afford watching anything during the week.

If you do not have to have a job right now do not get one. "Enjoy being a kid while you can, once you start working you can never stop". This was advice given to me by countless young people working while I was even younger. Now I am passing this advice down to you. Initially, I was the type of kid who could not wait until I was old enough to get a job and start making my own money. The way everyone consistently warned me about it scared me into listening. I am very glad I did. As it turned out, I did not have time during my school year anyway, and I really enjoyed my last summers of total free time. When you are older you will wish you had enjoyed your high school summers because you might not ever get that kind of break again. It is better to wait until the summer after your senior year to start working.

CHAPTER 11

TUTORIALS

I was not the "smartest" student in school. I spent a lot of my time in tutorials; especially for math classes. Unless you are gifted at understanding information the first time it is taught, you are going to have to spend some time in tutorials. If you know you do not understand something simply go to your teacher during their tutorial times so that you can understand it better. If your teacher does not provide tutorials then ask them if there is a time that you can get help before school, afterschool, or during your lunch period. Do not be afraid to ask for help from other students who are good at a subject that you are struggling in; I have asked help from my peers countless times. A majority of your peers will not go for extra help. Perhaps it is because they do not need it; however, you are not concerned about anyone but yourself in this regard. Do what you know you need to do in order to do well in class.

Being in athletics is no excuse not to go to tutorials. I was in athletics throughout the whole year every year, but I made time to go for extra help when I needed it. There were several times I missed the beginning of practice, but I made up for it. As long as you let your coach know when you are going to tutorials and follow any instructions given by them, they will not mind you going; they want you to do well in your classes so that you can participate. You are a student first and athlete second. Make sure you prioritize in that fashion.

In this technological age, help is never too far away. If you are having a hard time on something or have a question that needs to be answered immediately then the solution is simple: Google it! There are vast amounts of information available on the internet that covers almost every subject that you will be taking. There are even video tutorials on YouTube. You could possibly have all of your questions answered in seconds. There is literally no excuse not understanding material you are struggling to comprehend with such a variety of options available to you.

CHAPTER 12

THE CLASS ROOM

Class Room Participation

Academics are not all that a teacher is looking for in a student. A teacher also looks at how you participate and conduct yourself during class time. If you are a quiet person who does not really talk a lot the only thing you have to worry about is participating. Do not be afraid to answer a question when the teacher asks the class. Do not be afraid to stand out. A teacher actually appreciates when a student participates and interacts with their lesson plans. Some of you may not necessarily be "afraid" to participate it is just that you do not have a desire to. You need to get out of that frame of mind. You do not have to participate every time but at least once each class. Never be afraid to ask questions when appropriate either. If you have a question about a topic you are having trouble with chances are others in the class have the same question.

Now for those of you, like me, who like to talk a lot, your problem is going to be toning it down. There is a thing called "over" participating, or, in other terms, "sucking up". You want to come off as a student who is excited to participate but not as student who likes to "suck up" or thinks they know it all. What does that mean? Answer when you actually know the answer, but refrain from blurting out the answer if the teacher does not call on you. Do not raise your hand just because your teacher asked for someone to answer (when you do not even have an answer). If you know the answer then by all means answer it, but keep it simple; do not talk longer than you have to. Also watch the tone and inflections in your voice. Being able to hear how you sound may be difficult, but pay as close attention to it as much as possible. You may have the right answer, you may have kept it simple, but your attitude may cause you to sound unpleasant. Above all else, reframe from asking stupid questions. Yes, there is such a thing as stupid questions and do not let anyone convince you otherwise. Nothing irritates a teacher more than having to repeat information that was already given just because someone was not paying attention. Please do not ask questions you already know the answer to either.

Class Room Conduct

A teacher likes a hard working student who participates, but they love those students who are always behaving in class. This means that you are to follow all classroom rules. Write them in a booklet and memorize them if you need to. You cannot laugh and play around during class. It does not matter whether or not other kids are doing it; you need to make sure that you are not associated with disruptive students. A teacher notice's disruptive students, and though they might not always say anything, sometimes they have in their minds that they personally do not like those students. Keep in mind teachers are human too, and they do not like being disrespected any more than you do. Do not even mistreat those teachers that are "push overs"; they appreciate a student who does not misbehave and try to take advantage of them as the rest of the class does.

You are in that class room to learn, not to socialize (that may be hard to realize for some of you); so save all the joking and playing for before and after class. What will help you accomplish this is if you do not sit with your friends during class. "What?! Not sit with my friends?! That's crazy!" You cannot sit with your friends and not want to talk and joke around at some point. You will then become both distracted as well as a distraction within the class. It does not matter what "other" kids are doing around you. What matters is what YOU are doing.

I recommend sitting in the front of all your classes. Teachers already know that the students who choose to be in the back tend to be the most disruptive. They also know that those few students that sit in the front everyday are the ones who are serious and want to learn. This can put you in good graces with that teacher while keeping yourself from being a disruption in the class. Some teachers might have a seating chart. If it is difficult to stay focused where you are assigned, then wait after class and ask your teacher if you can be assigned to another location (preferably the front). If they say no then do not worry about it; just do your best to stay focused.

Why is Class Room Conduct so Important?

There is an old saying, "Don't burn your bridges." You do not want to burn a bridge once you cross it because you never know when you may need to go back in that direction. When you need an extra point for the class or a recommendation letter to get into an organization and or college, a teacher can decide whether or not they want to do that for you. Always make sure you are behaving properly so that teachers are eager to help you when you need it most.

A teacher also notices when you are putting in a lot of work. If there is just one point or two that you need to get an A or even a B in the class they might bump you up. They never have to do that. Teachers have control of how they do their grading;

they could possible change their grading scale just to help those hard working students out. However, it is not guaranteed they will do that. Teachers are also not required to round your average. For example, if you have a 79.99999 that teacher is not required to give you an 80. So if you are one of those students who slacked off and was constantly disruptive, that teacher could very well choose to give you that 79 which you earned. If you are a good student then they could decide to round your grade to an 80.

It is impossible to be the "perfect" student. At times you can make mistakes and be disruptive to the class. You may at some point be disrespectful to a teacher. What helps you make up for your mistakes, which most people have too much pride to do, is to apologize. I was never disrespectful to a teacher, but at times I did misbehave and disrupt class. It was not as bad as other kids, however, when you are distinguishing yourself as a good student teachers tend to look at you differently and expect more from you. If they do not already expect more from you then give them more to expect. Owning up to your mistakes is one of the best ways of accomplishing this; it also shows maturity. I myself had to apologize a few times to teachers. What gives your apology more strength is by also including that you will never do it again. Of course you need to make sure you keep that promise. It means a lot to a teacher when you show maturity and apologize when you are wrong.

CHAPTER 13

THE SCHOOL

School Conduct

Your good conduct does not end in the class room. You have to remain in good conduct as long as you are on campus. You want to obtain and maintain the reputation of a good student. Administrators, principals, and even future teachers are watching. One thing you may have not realized yet is that teachers and administrators talk to one another. They will warn future teachers about some of the students that are disruptive.

Be careful who you choose to hang around before, in between, and after classes; even during lunch. Distance yourselves away from those who tend to be pranksters. Distance yourselves from those who "rebel" against authority. These are the kids many may think are cool and very popular, however, more than likely, by the end of high school they would not have amounted to much of anything. You may be thinking that you can behave yourself when you are around certain people. Though you may or may not act like those you are around, everyone else views you as part of that group. Whatever reputation the group has you will have also. Choose your company wisely. You do not want to be labeled as a trouble maker by association.

Addressing Adults/Authority

Always show respect to adults, even if they do not respect you; yes, you read that correctly. These include those that are in authority (administrators and teachers), maintenance workers, and janitors. It is not necessary to have extended conversations with everyone, just simply be respectful and greet them if you make eye contact. Say things like "Good morning" "Good after noon" or a simple "Hi. How are you?" You do not necessarily have to greet everyone you walk by (just on occasion). Let it be natural. If they greet you first, open your mouth and respond verbally.

There is another matter that desperately needs to be discussed. When you are being addressed by an adult ALWAYS say "Yes ma'am" "No ma'am" Or "Yes sir" "No sir". I want you to practice that if you are not use to replying in this manner. These are things that your fellow peers will not say; because of that, it will not go unnoticed. You do not realize how much an adult appreciates a respectable young person; they are a dying breed. You never know how a certain adult can help you along on your road to success; make it easy for them to want to help you.

Another important thing to always remember not to do is to "buck" authority. Even if there might be a misunderstanding on the adult's part you are to always remain respectful. If there is an issue you can wait until your parents or guardian come and handle it. Never speak as if you have the authority of an adult; you do not. You are a child not an adult, so do not overstep your bounds (though at times it can be very tempting). If you over step your bounds, you can easily make matters worse for yourself. If a teacher or other authority is in the wrong, let them win the battle, then bring your parents back with you to win the war. It is all about having a respectful and effective strategy.

CHAPTER 14

THE SOCIAL REALM

Until now, I have stressed the importance of working hard and staying focused. That does not mean you cannot enjoy all high school has to offer. High school may not be all fun and games, but it would not be high school without some fun and games. I worked hard to become valedictorian, but I also ran for other positions while there. I became class president for my last two years and I participated in organizations like National Honors

Society. One thing colleges do look for is an active student. When they see that you were involved in clubs, organizations (especially when you are an officer), and sports, they take note that you were a leader and not an average student. Though it may not be the most critical aspect colleges look at, in a highly competitive school where most applicants have the same scores as you, being an active student can push you ahead of the rest.

Aside from being valedictorian I was also homecoming prince my junior year and prom king my senior year. That was not planned; I just ran for the fun of it all. Though colleges do not take these accomplishments into consideration it is still fun. Do not be afraid to put yourself out there and do not be afraid to lose. I lost several times when I ran for things, but that never stopped me from trying nor did it prevent me from having a good time. The only way to fully maximize your high school years is to test your limits and see how far you can go. You may surprise yourself.

Clubs/Organizations

If you want to max out your high school experience I recommend joining an organization or club. Whatever your particular interest is, if there is a club for it you should join it. You get to meet new people that share similar interests whom you may have never met outside of the organization; not to mention that it looks nice on a college application. If you really want to impress colleges you should do your best to become an officer of that particular organization (if they have them). The most prestigious organizations to be in are student government and the National Honors Society.

National Honors Society, in short, is the organization where the hardest working students are chosen to join. You have to meet certain qualifications in order to be eligible to join. If you get in, it will look very well on your college application (which you want).

Home Coming and all that Jazz

Though running for these positions is not actually beneficial to your college career, it is still exciting! I started off by running for duke my freshmen year. I did not win, but it actually got my face and name visible to my classmates. It boosted my reputation and allowed my class and the rest of the school to know who I was. This helped pave the way for other things that I ran for. If you do decide to run then go all out: put up posters, banners, flyers or any other creative techniques you can think of. Above anything, win or lose, just have fun! One key thing to remember is that if you win early on then it is possible that your likelihood of winning again in the future will decrease. People sometimes get "tired" of the same person winning and will vote for someone one else; do not let that small possibility stop you. Win or lose run as many times as you wish.

How I Became President

There might be some of you who want to know my strategy to becoming president. There is no sure way for you to become president, but I have a few tips that can help. One thing that helped me was that I was always a sociable individual who talked to everyone. I never had one specific group that I was associated with. I made friends and acquaintances from multiple groups. I never mistreated anyone either; you should never mistreat anyone, even if the rest of your "friends" do. If you want to be president of your class, you have to get to know your classmates and let them get to know you. One thing you need to know about people is that not everyone will like you. Some will dislike you for no apparent reason. You are not out to make everyone like you, you are out there to be known and respected. Some people, no matter what, will not like you; do not waste your energy on trying. Respect carries a lot more weight than someone liking you. Even if someone did not like you, but they still respected you, they may still vote for you regardless.

Other than being sociable, I had another strategy. My freshman year I did not run for president right away; I ran for a lower position so that I could ensure that I got in and became familiar with the operation. The person who was running for president was very popular, and it would not have been in my best interest to run against that person right away. Even if I won, it could have worked to my disadvantage. As I stated previously, when you win right away, it can have a negative effect on you winning again; especially when you do not know what you are doing. The next year I ran for vice president to put myself closer to my goal.

The main quality that allowed me to become president and stay president for two years was that I cared for my classmates and wanted to do great things for them. You have to have a passion for your class. Most, if not all other officers (including the same president), at the time, only wanted their positions so that it would look good on their college application. There was constant discussion about doing things for the class, but no one was taking the initiative to actually accomplish anything. My sophomore year as vice president, I planned and orchestrated a field trip for my class. At my school field trips for sophomores was unheard of! This was something that was predominantly done for seniors, but they never said it could only be for seniors. I included the entire class on it so that they could decide where they wanted to go. As a result of accomplishing this all other officers finally came together for the good of our class. Needless to say, I won the presidency that year by a land slide. I did not stop there. My junior year we received a new principal. This restricted our ability to organize special events. I did not want our class to go out empty handed, so I did the next best thing. I set the wheels in motion so that our junior class could receive our own unique senior shirt at the end of the year. Again, it was unheard of for juniors to receive their senior shirts before their actual senior year. The rest of the class was again included and they loved it! By my senior year we heard constant voices from our class of where they wanted to go for prom and so I set out to make sure that it was available. For many years, seniors had gone to the same prom location; we wanted something special.

Of course we gave them more options but I made sure that the main location was available. We managed to get that location (which the class did vote on). We were the only senior class to actually have that special location (even after us). The only way to show your class that you care for them is by letting them see just how hard you are working for them.

The final attribute I want to mention is having leadership capabilities. Even through all of my accomplishments, I still could not have done it all without the help of my officers. I knew that I had to be a leader in order to bring them together to accomplish great things. The only way we could do that was to have order within our organization. As president, you cannot back down and allow others to bulldoze you. You have to be strong. There were times where I had to make difficult decisions, but I made them in efforts to maintain order. As a leader, you have to be willing to say and do things others are too afraid to do. Of course I am not implying that you do something that you should not or even become disrespectful, but at the same time not being weak and passive. You have to remain stern at times. If you do not have leadership capability, it will be difficult to be an effective president.

As I stated before, there is no definite way of becoming president; use this information as a start. Some methods may not work for you. You do not necessarily have to utilize my entire strategy. You have to figure out what works best for you, and that is part of being a leader.

PART 3:
PREPARING FOR
COLLEGE

Chapter 15

Final preparations

Now that you know how to take care of your business for the next four years, you still have some final preparations to make. Applying for college and having your financial aid in order still needs to be addressed. Though most of the subjects discussed in this section will not be a priority until your senior year, there are some things you will benefit from by starting years in advance (like applying for

scholarships).

CHAPTER 16

FINANCIAL AID

One of the most crucial things you need to have in place before entering college is your financial aid. You should not have to worry about this until your junior and or senior year, but you still need to be ready.

Financial aid is the money granted to you by a second party to help pay for your college. Financial aid comes from scholarships, grants, and loans. Unlike loans, scholarships and grants are money given to you that you do not have to pay back later; you want as many scholarships and grants as possible so that you can escape from debt when you come out of college. If you receive anything that tells you that you have to pay to receive any information about financial aid and scholarships it is a scam. Information and applying for financial aid is always free. There are scams out there that target juniors and seniors and they make a lot of money because parents and students do not realize it until it is too late. Now that you know this you should not become a victim.

Chapter 17

Loans

In short, a loan is money that you borrow.
All you need to know about loans to start you off is
that you will eventually have to pay that amount of
money back with interest. There are many types of
loans. More than likely, you have heard about
student loans. Loans are there to help you pay for
school when you need it. I recommend doing your
best to get as many scholarships and grants as you
possibly can to avoid having to get a loan. If you do

need more financial aid to pay for your education,

loans are there to assist you. Speak with your

counselor for more advice and information about

loans.

Chapter 18

Scholarships

A scholarship is simply free money. Most of you have probably heard of people receiving scholarships for being really smart (academic scholarship) or really good at a sport (athletic scholarships); these are often awarded through the college that accepts you. These are not the only scholarships available. There are literally millions of other scholarships waiting to be awarded; you just have to apply for as many as possible in hopes that you will receive one or more. The more scholarships you receive the less money that comes out of you or your family's pocket.

How do I get a Scholarship?

You have to apply for it. Keep in mind that you are competing against other students who are applying for the same scholarships. Different scholarships have a different application process. You impress those you are applying to, and they help sponsor you to go to college. That money will be used to help you pay for any college expenses. If you have enough scholarship money, it can even take care of your on-campus housing.

How do I apply for a Scholarship?

In many cases, you will not be able to apply for scholarships until you are at least a junior. You should still check and see if there are scholarships you can apply for before then; you never know if some scholarships allow you to apply sooner. You can go online to research scholarships. It can be very tedious, but definitely worth your time. You can also speak to your counselor for advice on finding scholarships if you do not know where to start. Do not be afraid to ask teachers either; they may have knowledge of scholarships that others do not. You can even ask your bank if they have any scholarships that you could apply for. Scholarships are scattered everywhere around you; you just have to be observant. If you start looking for them years in advanced (even if you cannot apply for them yet) you will be organized and prepared when the time comes. You will already know what scholarships to apply for and when to apply. Not only does this make your life easier, it increases your opportunities for more scholarships.

How should I apply for scholarships?

Apply for as many scholarships as you possibly can! You never know which ones you will receive. Just because you apply does not mean that you automatically get it. There is a lot of competition against other students and it may not only depend on just having a high GPA; you may have to write a really good essay. Applying earlier than the rest of your peers is the best time to do it. Some students are not even aware of this until later in their junior years; so you are, hopefully, already ahead. The sooner you apply increases the chances of you receiving scholarships.

Do not make the mistake of overlooking scholarships that offer a low amount of money. This is a mistake many students make. Students only focus on the few scholarships with the most money. What they do not realize is that by applying to all the small scholarships, if they get them, they add up to a lot of money. Since many students make this mistake the competition will not be as much. Of course you should still apply for the scholarships with the most money as well. If you receive enough scholarship money you could actually have money left over in which you can use any way you want! You could have thousands of dollars in your bank account to do as you please.

CHAPTER 19

GRANTS

Grants are predominately given out through

the government (either national or state level), your

college, or an organization. Unlike loans you do not

have to pay back any amount of the money given to

you.

How do I apply for a grant?

In many cases, government grants are given

through what is called FAFSA (Free Application for

Federal Student Aid). It is an online application you must fill out in order for the government to see how much government financial aid can be given to you.

The amount of financial aid that you can receive depends mostly on your household income and the cost to go to the college that you will be attending. They will use this information to calculate the amount of financial aid that will be given you. You could still receive grants from your college or any other organization/foundation that offers them. Similar to scholarships, you will have to apply for them. Ask your counselor for advice on how to begin your search.

About FAFSA

You will not have to apply until the second semester of your senior year. In order to receive priority funding you must have your application completed and submitted by a certain date of your senior year. The sooner you apply for your FAFSA, the higher your chances of receiving the maximum funding. Ask your counselor for further information regarding FAFSA and deadline dates.

Chapter 20

Applying for College

Applying for college is one of the busiest, heartbreaking, and joyous times in high school. It is during this time that you actually reach out to the colleges of your dreams in hopes they will accept you. It may be heartbreaking because the first college you hoped to go to may not accept you. It will definitely be joyous when a college does accept you and provides you with funding.

I asked earlier in the book that you take a look at the colleges you wished to attend your freshman year and find out what the requirements are to be accepted. By the time you start applying for college hopefully you will have met those requirements. You will start applying for college either the middle of the first semester of your senior year (to apply early) or it will be in the beginning of your second semester. I recommend that you apply to at least 4 different colleges; you may not get your first choice. One thing to keep in mind is that you will have to actually pay to just apply to different colleges. Certain colleges, particularly private colleges, will have a higher application fee. In any case, make sure you check and recheck your deadlines; it would be a shame for you not to get into the college you want because you mixed up the due dates.

Applying Early

If you decided to, you can actually apply early for college. There is a great benefit in doing this. If you apply early you will get first priority over other students that apply later. This means that you have a higher chance of being accepted into that particular college. You may also be able to increase your chances of getting the maximum amount of funding from that college.

Though this sounds good there can be some draw backs. You would have to send in your GPA and SAT scores as is. This means that your GPA and your SAT/ACT scores have to meet the requirements of the college by the early start of your senior year. It may benefit your chances still to boost your GPA and SAT scores more with another semester. However, if your scores are already great, then you may have nothing to worry about.

Sometimes there are certain rules/plans that may force you to go to that college if you are accepted. You may also be only allowed to apply early to one college. This will prevent you from looking and applying to other colleges. Make sure you talk with your counselor in advance to determine if applying early is right for you. I would only recommend applying early if the college is highly competitive (like Harvard and Yale) and it is the college that you know for a fact that it is where you want to go. If you are trying to find the college that gives you the most money then applying early may not be for you.

Applying by the Normal Deadline

Applying by the normal deadlines can be the safest way to go. Of course the amount of competition is greater, but you have more time to raise your scores. You can compare all the colleges you were accepted to in order to figure out which would be the best fit for you. You will not have to rush and have the pressure of getting your SAT/ACT scores in a shorter period of time. It is definitely the more relaxing plan but you still have to make sure you turn in your applications on time. Make sure you check and recheck all application deadlines. If you are unclear about the application process or requirements speak with your counselor

and or the college directly.

PART 4: YEARLY CHECK LIST

CHAPTER 21

YEARLY CHECK LIST AND TIPS

Now you have the information that you need which will help you to be successful in high school. This is still a lot of information to process so I have drawn up a summary checklist for each year. The information listed is not arranged in any particular order. Not everything is included in the check list; it is only the things that I think should be a first priority. You will still need to go back and read over the sections to maximize the use of this book.

Freshman Year

1. Go to your school with your parent or guardian during the summer, before school starts, to adjust your schedule (about 3 weeks before school starts).

2. Start thinking about any organizations you may want to join later

3. Figure out an everyday study routine that works well for you.

4. If you want to have a little fun why not run for home coming court? Even if you lose the experience is still great. Who knows, getting your face out there may come in handy in the years to come.

5. Develop good relationships with your teachers. Be respectful at all times.

6. Try to venture out. Get to know your fellow peers. Try not to stay in one group. The ability to connect with most of your surroundings is an important social skill.

7. Think about the colleges you want to go to. Check what the requirements are to get in.

Sophomore Year

1. At the beginning of every new semester go to the registers office and ask for your transcript. This keeps you up to date on your GPA

standing. Sometimes they may even provide your ranking.

2. Make sure you remember to visit your school to adjust your schedule before the summer ends.

3. If you have not joined any organizations, choose one to join that you like the most. If you have the time you can to join more than one organization. Maybe try running for an officer's position (if they have it).

4. Talk to your counselor and ask about SAT/ACT prep classes that you can take outside of school.

5. Do not forget to check your GPA each semester.

6. Now is a great time to start asking and looking around for scholarships. Talk with your counselor or teachers for advice on how to start.

Junior Year

1. Have your schedule prepared during the summer.
2. If you are in an organization and have not run for an office yet this year will be your last chance. So go for it!
3. By now you should have already taken SAT/ACT prep classes on your own. I recommend by the end of the year that you take the Pre-SAT/ACT; check and see if your school will be

providing it for you. If you plan on applying to college early you may want to consider taking the actual test instead.

4. Do not forget to check your GPA and ranking.

5. Start looking for and applying for scholarships now. Go to your counselor for further assistance. Apply for as many as you can.

6. REMEMBER: If someone is telling you that you have to pay to apply or receive information for scholarships or other financial aid it is a scam.

7. Check all requirements for the colleges you want to apply to and see where you currently stand. If you

intend on applying early you should be very close (if not already) to meeting all requirements by the end of your junior year.

Senior Year

1. Make sure your schedule is fixed before school starts.
2. Continue to look for scholarships and keep applying. Apply to as many as you can find!
3. You should have taken SAT/ACT prep courses for the past 2 years now. You want to try to take the SAT and ACT as many times as you can afford to by the end of December. Even if you have the

required score, having a higher score will help you stand out above all other students; higher scores are always better especially when applying to Ivy League colleges.

4. Remember: The first semester may be the only semester that actually count towards your GPA, but if you start doing poorly the second semester colleges will still see that and it will have a negative impact. Do not catch "senioritis".

5. Either before or after the first semester you should have all the materials you need to start applying to colleges. Make sure you apply to at least 4 colleges. You never know

who will accept you. Even when one college does accept you, there may be a college that is willing to offer you more scholarship money than the others. You want to strongly consider going to the college that offers you the most money.

6. In the second semester, if you want, you can change out of some of the extra AP courses you loaded your schedule with that first semester and replace them with easier courses (or perhaps the left over classes you need to graduate with). That is actually exactly what I did; it made my last semester very relaxing.

7. Make sure you complete and submit your FAFSA before the primary funding deadline. Go to your counselor and ask what you need to do to complete it in time.

PART 5: CONCLUSION

CHAPTER 22

CONCLUSION

I have covered all the information that

assisted me in getting through high school, but it is

not everything. There is always something new that

you can learn. Listen to teachers and administrators

as they can always provide you with new

knowledge and wisdom. There is no such thing as a

"perfect" plan. Some situations you simply cannot

plan for. Reading this book will not guarantee that

you will be valedictorian, and it does not mean you

will win a popularity contest. I am not saying this to discourage you from trying your best; I am telling you this so that you will not be frustrated when you do your best. Never beat yourself up when you give one-hundred percent and things do not work out the way you hoped. Some classes I did not do as well as wanted to do, but I never got too frustrated because I knew I did the best that I could.

You do not have to read this book at the beginning of your eighth grade year to be successful. You could have discovered this book at the beginning of your junior year and still use pointers and tips that can help you maximize the rest of your time in high school. Whatever you do, do not give up if you fall short of your goals. Always pick yourself up and keep at it!

Some advice and instructions given in this book do not have to stop in high school. It all amounts to how badly you want to be successful in anything you do. You have to have a plan, you have to be open to the right advice, you have to follow the correct advice given to you, you have to have a good attitude, and you have to put one-hundred percent of your effort into whatever it is you want to do. Do not allow anything to hold you back, even yourself. Eliminate all doubt and fears on what you can accomplish. In my younger years, I would have never imagined I would become valedictorian. Before high school, I had always been the laid back type of student. I did ok, but I never showed any signs of applying myself. I enjoyed playing around! One of my elementary teachers was not fond of me and a friend because of our behavior; imagine her surprise when we visited our old school years later and she saw that I was valedictorian and he was the salutatorian. My point is that others, as well as yourself, may not always realize the potential that you have. Anything that you set your mind to and anything you want just as badly as you desire to breathe you can achieve it.

As this book comes to a close, I would like to take the time to bust a myth about high school that I talked about in my graduation speech: your high school years are NOT the best years of your life. At least they do not have to be. High school may be the last of the easiest years of your life, but you have so much more to look forward to. Set new goals for yourself, and do not allow your peers or yourself to distract you from those goals. The road to success does not stop in high school, it continues on for the rest of your life. Also, if you plan to go to college, do NOT take a break from school after you graduate; many have come to regret that decision. Instead, push through and finish college. I want to wish you all the best of luck in high school, college, and the rest of your life. Thank you for allowing me to be an influence on your life and I hope that it makes the world of difference. Now a new chapter in your own life begins.

BIBLIOGRAPHY

http://apcentral.collegeboard.com/home

"College Board." *AP Central*. N.p., n.d. Web. 10 June 2014.

http://www.fcps.org/cms/lib02/MD01000577/Centri city/Domain/28/UnderstandingGPAs.pdf

Term Grades Are Given At The End Of Each 9 Week Term (Also Called A Quarter Or Marking Period). A. "Understanding Grade Point Average (GPA)." *Understanding Grade Point Average (GPA)* (n.d.): n. pag. *Frederic County Public Schools*. FCPS. Web. 10 June 2014.

http://www.collegeconfidential.com/

"College Admissions, Search, and Financial Aid Help from College Confidential." *College Admissions, Search, and Financial Aid Help from College Confidential*. N.p., n.d. Web. 10 June 2014.

http://www.princetonreview.com/sat-act.aspx

"The SAT vs. the ACT | SAT ACT Comparison." *The SAT vs. the ACT*. Princetonreview, n.d. Web. 10 June 2014.

https://studentaid.ed.gov/fafsa/next-steps/how-calculated

"Wondering How the Amount of Your Federal Student Aid Is Determined?" *How Aid Is Calculated*. Federal Student Aid, n.d. Web. 10 June 2014.

https://www.scholarships.com/financial-aid/college-scholarships/scholarship-information/scholarship-opportunities/

"Scholarship Opportunities." *Scholarship Information*. Scholarships.com, n.d. Web. 10 June 2014.

https://bigfuture.collegeboard.org/get-in/applying-101/the-facts-about-applying-early-is-it-right-for-you

"The Facts About Applying to College Early: Is It Right for You?" *The Facts About Applying to College Early: Is It Right for You?* College Board, n.d. Web. 10 June 2014.

Made in the USA
Lexington, KY
31 January 2018